Thick and Thin

Written by Alison Hawes

Ken has a thick wool scarf.
The thick wool keeps out the cold.

Hema has a thin top.
The thin fabric keeps her cool.

Bev is painting with a thick brush.
She likes to paint monsters.

Mel has a thin brush.
She is painting red dots.

Lee has a thin plastic mac.
It keeps out the wet.

Mark has a thick coat.
It feels soft.

Jack has a thick pen.
He did this coil pattern with it.

Anan likes zigzag patterns.
She gets a thin pen.

Kim has a pet mouse.
It has a long, thin tail.

Kevin has lots of pets.
His hamster has a short, thick tail.

Ben likes big, thick chips.
He gets them from a fish and
chip shop.

Sam likes long, thin pasta.
Her dad cooks it.

Thick

Thin

Thin

Thick

Thick

Thin

Thick

Thin

Thin

Thick

Thick

Thin

:paw: Ideas for reading :paw:

Written by Kelley Taylor
Educational Consultant

Reading objectives:
- use phonic knowledge to decode regular words and read them aloud accurately
- read some common irregular words
- read and understand simple sentences
- demonstrate understanding when talking with others about what they have read

Communication and language objectives:
- listen attentively in a range of situations
- listen to stories, and respond to what they hear with relevant comments, questions or actions
- express themselves effectively, showing awareness of listeners' needs

Curriculum links: Knowledge and understanding of the world; Creative development; Physical development

Focus phonemes: th (thick, thin), oo (wool, cook), v (names Bev, Kevin), oi (coil)

Other new phonemes: ar, er, ou, sh, th (this), ee, z, oo (cool)

Fast words: a, the, her, he, to, she, of

Word count: 147

Build a context for reading

- Write the words that include the focus phonemes *th*, *oo*, *v* and *oi* on a small whiteboard and ask the group to read them, blending aloud if they need to.

- After reading the words that feature the short *oo* sound (*wool*, *cook*) write up the word *cool* and make sure the children tell the difference between the long and short *oo* sound.

- Before reading, check that children understand the meanings of a selection of the following words: *pattern*, *pasta*, *fabric*, *scarf*, *zigzag*, *hamster* and *plastic mac*. Ask the group to decide if these objects are thick or thin. Encourage debate as the children try to organise their ideas.

Understand and apply reading strategies

- Read pp2–3 together, blending along the words. If necessary, remind the group of the discussion involving tricky words like *fabric* to read them.

- As the children continue to read independently, prompt them to remember the pairs of thick and thin objects. Say that you will be asking them to talk about them at the end.